Poetic Outlines of a Teenager

Jessica Holden

Poetic Outlines of a Teenager

For Chantel- mentor turned legal guardian turned sister turned guardian angel. Thank you!

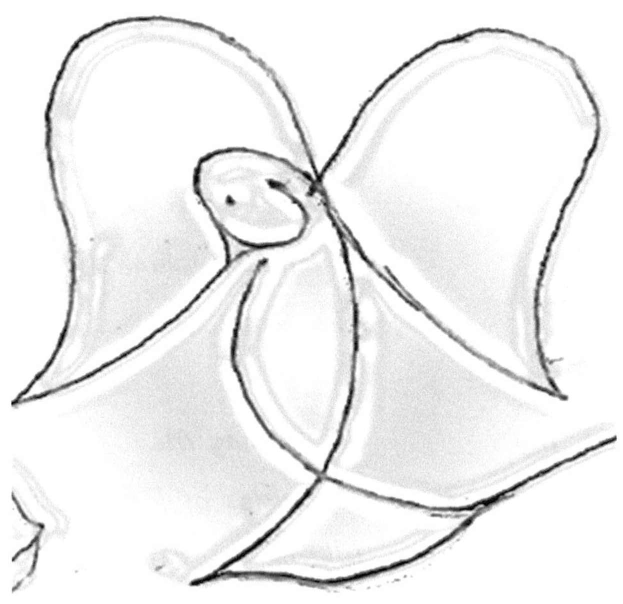

Contents

Introduction ... 1
Teaser... 3

I· (S)heroes
A True Queen... 5
Real Woman... 8
My Unborn... 11
Best Friend... 13
Hero... 17

II· My Society, My Reality
Reach... 23
Society's Mirror... 28
Reflections... 30
It's Time... 34
The Home Front... 36

III· Detour to Feelings
Appetite... 41
I Want To... 43
Careless Paint Strokes 45
I Want to Laugh... 47
The Game... 51

IV· Finding Me
Chronicles of Poetry...53
Whispers... 59
Prostitute of Poetry 63
Life... 67
Know Thyself... 68

Introduction

I'm a firm believer that writing poetry is something that cannot be taught. Sure, you can learn how to format words into a haiku or sonnet or put words together because they sound good and call it poetry, but without emotion words are worthless. Poetry represents feeling, a moment, a dream, a failure, life! Poetry IS life and if I'm not mistaken there is no manual in place to teach folks how to live.

I began writing my own life reflections when I entered the foster care system at 10. Words were the easiest way to construct a safe haven in the midst of turmoil. By 6th grade I was competing in speech competitions (and winning). It wasn't until my 7th grade teacher took me to my first open mic that I saw poetry come to life. Each poet gave a piece of themselves to the audience, serving up a platter of passion I wanted all to myself. But it wasn't my recipe. I realized my life was not ideal but I needed to dig deeper, explore myself, and share it with others. So here we are. I've compiled 11 years of poetry, a testament to my ever-changing life (and ever-growing vocabulary). I'm always inspired by the work of others, so hopefully you'll find a piece of inspiration within these pages. Enjoy :-)

- Jessica

The Teaser

Poetry and I have been engaged for quite some time now
But as of late we haven't been able to set a date
I'd like to be married on the date we met, that faithful night at a coffee shop on the North side
She feels the day we conceived our first poem would be more appropriate
I want to wed on the sunny shores of my conscience
Poetry wants the I dos to take place in the wild jungles of her soul
Poetry and I have been engaged for some time now
We have yet to set a date

(S)heroes

A True Queen

Once, long ago, there was a queen
Bejeweled from head to toe
Only the most foolish didn't know that
She reigned supreme
Overseeing a kingdom where time stood still
Power was in the palm of her hand
And only changed at her will
Yet, in every crevice of her soul
She felt an approaching destruction
In which she had no control
All around her, her subjects began to stray from the community
After all
Craps shootin' and drug dealin' were more appealing then
Peace and prosperity
And it seemed that where unity once used to be
Her subjects could be found fighting over trivial misunderstandings
Brandishing abandonment into the land
That the Queen's family had seen over since the world was just sand
And soon the poor Queen found herself hustlin' to make ends meet
Pawning her crown and jewels in defeat

She stepped off her throne
And used everyone last of her bones
And scrubbed the floor of those who once served her
And seem being a Queen didn't seem to please
Employers who viewed her resume`
She dropped down to her knees
Asking for strength from her ancestors
Fearing this day
The day she would have to profit of the creation God made
She was stripped of her innocence and now felt alone
Especially when she found out
She'd be having a future hustler of her own
No, she couldn't fathom the idea
That she was a Queen
But her little princess would never be known as anything
Except a good time with legs
And as much as she begged
To reach the red light of her life
She cried a river full of tears
And as much as she tried to fight it
She gazed at this River of Humiliation
She looked past her pain, her fears, and her hurt
And scooped up something more valuable than gold
She sat amongst the banks caressing her soul
Yes, she still had a soul

Allowing her to be bold
Enough to go back and receive an education
As she, and her newborn practiced patience
She purchased a small palace of her own
And made enough money so her daughter
A princess
Would never feel how cold a former kingdom could become
And maybe to some
She lost her riches and fame
But her trials and tribulations taught her that she did have a name
And she did have a place
She would teach her daughter of a long forgotten place
Where love and peace were always in reach
And that it was in her blood to reign supreme
Some may call her a warrior
Survivor
But she is worthy of one true title
Even though her scars may showcase a fighter
In the seams of her soul
And the conscience of her being
She possessed the spirit
Of a true Queen

Real Woman

I am a real woman
I am a real woman with real goals
Real spirit and real soul
My mother, a real woman, said,
"Behold! The realest of the real is here!"

See, I've been through such pain
Cried more tears than it's rained
My life ignites such flames
That only a real woman, this woman, can contain

Once upon a time, there was a girl
Enjoying her Barbie Dolls and teddy bears
She heard a knock at the door that would change her world
Opened it up to see Life standing there
Snatched out of her only home
Leaving Teddy and Barbie behind
Thrown in a pit of unmentionables
It was enough to make the realest man teary-eyed

Looked for support to find none there
'Cuz in the real world it doesn't exist
Went from a ten year old kid to a ten year old phenomenon

Packed up her real emotions to find her own bliss

But bliss is easy to misunderstand
Through all the hurt and lies
She continued to rise
Until something, rather someone, caught her eye
The reincarnation of a real man

See, like Adam needed Eve
Like husband needs wife
A real man needs a real woman
This man needed her in his life

But what this man needed was a reality check
He thought he was the sun, and she revolved around this man
Took away her real words, real feelings, real goals
And replaced them with his own plan

She lost her voice and strength
Waiting for his beck and call
With him being the man, controlling everything
There was no use for her at all

However, once a real woman is created
A real woman remains
She emerged from his world

And brought along her real pain
Grabbed this fool by the collar
As she led the way
She told him how Life knocked on her door
And she had no choice but to let it in
But out was the only direction for this almost man
Their beginning was his end

Once again...
We are real women
We use real words
And only real men know how to be real about theirs
and take it
We are real women
Real flow, real soul, real bold
Really comfortable about the real us
Not defined by what society says
Only the real remain
Watered down versions are no more

My Unborn

My unborn child
Let us pray
After nine months before that special day
If God may
The world will be a better place
BUT WATCH OUT NOW!
Momma can do a lot
But she can't protect you forever
And never, Lord never
Could the nation, and the world, and the universe
Get so lopsided, crooked, and cracked
But it did
And don't worry
You can step on a crack
And you'll never break your mother's back
But if you and I slide apart
'Cuz you paid no heed to my words
You done broke my heart
Remember
You're my future's future
And if one day
If it's not ripped or crumpled
You can read this
And with your little hands and mind
You can comprehend

That's from your mother's side of the family
But if my words go unspoken
And my verses unread
Go ahead
Because I have a feeling that you
My unborn child
Have already set a positive foot into the dirt road
Get a good grip on life
Like momma had to do
And move on up
'Till the air is thin
And then begin
To carve "Dreams", and "Hopes", and "Wishes" into the sky
Why?
'Cuz like I said
You're my future's future
And I want you to make changes as soon as possible
And it seems like a lot of pressure
But don't worry
'Cuz there are plenty of future mommas
Doing the same thing
And the children will be the backbone
I just hope you take notice of this rare support
One more thing
Welcome to your world
If you chose to claim it

Best Friend

Last night I had a dream
And in this dream, I saw all of my dreams
Rather, our dreams go down the drain
Maybe I should explain
See, it has always been me and my best friend
Crazy to some friends, but my number one friend
She's that kick it friend
The only one out the group who sticks to the plan friend
She's my main man
And I love her

See me and my best friend have this theory
That if we steer clear of misery, gunshots, and prison
We'll be able to live out our visions
We always talked about going into business together
Cuz' that's what best friends do
She's going to be the mastermind
And I'll be the one who makes sure everything goes through
And even though we don't know exactly what we're going to do
We're going to do it together
Cuz' that's what best friends do

And we love each other

Even though she's only a year older, she's like a mother
She just teaches me things a momma wouldn't normally teach
Like hot sauce really does go on everything
But I teach her stuff too
Like if you study hard enough you can get an A on anything
And that whatever she believes in, she can achieve
Because best friends are forever
And our love will get us through

But see negativity can sense that
All of the evil tries to pull us in
But we're too tight for that, you can't break us apart
Cuz' we have deep love for one another
And our love is all we got

But all the love in the world can't make me forget
It can't make me forget how her body collapsed to the ground
As the pistol fired its final round
Feet shuffling, kids screaming, dogs barking, and boys become men

As they grab their guns and fire away
But that didn't matter...·
That didn't matter because my best friend's blood was on my hands
And with that blood flowed hopes and dreams and wishes
Our hopes, our dreams, our wishes
Into the grass where her body laid
People try to pull me away
But I can't go
I need to see her face
So I can tell her how much I love her
And how I'll keep that love with me forever...

I wake up, chilled with sweat covering me like little diamonds
Confused by what just occurred
Because in my dream I reach for her
And turn her over, but she not there

I saw your best friend
I saw your mother
I saw your father, and your sister, and your brother
I saw aunties and uncles, baby girls and little boys, and everyone you've ever loved
But most importantly, I saw you

I saw your hopes and your wishes and your dreams flow into the grass
I saw your family in tears as your body was covered with plastic
Tossed into the ambulance like yesterday's trash

We watch ourselves die everyday
Wrapped up in shoulda, woulda, couldas
Our fingers on the trigger
Yet we refuse to remove them
We prefer to murder ourselves before the threshold, than to venture beyond it
But like the love between me and my best friend
You have it within yourselves
Give yourselves the chance to live
You have yet to discover the potential of what you can be
Without faith the only title you'll receive
Is R·I·P

Hero

Danielle didn't expect it
Being a hero isn't something you plan for
But she is
Not the hero we dream to be
Because to be her you have to live through nightmares
But believe me when I tell you
She is

Her mother didn't give a damn
She used to but the past is the past
And at last she found herself a hero
Willing to provide for her mistakes-
Her children of past false heroes
But Danielle considered him a zero
A weirdo
Something wasn't right
He crept past her and her sister's bedrooms at night
Floorboards squeaking, pleading for Danielle to flee
But Danielle wasn't fleeing
She was dreaming...dreaming...peacefully
Of a life with her mommy and daddy
So happy so hopeful so normal
Because that's all she ever wanted to be

But something told her Mr. Zero wasn't

Soon mommy turned him from a hero to a husband
And Danielle grew from a child to a budding woman
Assuming her mommy would explain
But mommy didn't
Too busy trying to entertain her husband
Who wasn't so focused on her as her was Danielle
Who no longer felt
But knew something wasn't right

So Danielle went to go tell mommy
But mommy was no longer mommy
Mommy was now wife
And wife didn't have time for Danielle
Who was trying to steal her husband
Or so she thought
So Danielle tried to pretend Mr. Zero didn't exist
But Mr. Zero did
And Mr. Zero knew everything
Like when she took showers so he could barge right in
Saying it was an accident
Staring at her glistening skin
And when he began to take Danielle to school
Because wife refused to
He began to say nasty things that Danielle wasn't use to
But who could she turn to if mommy who was wife didn't care?

Then Danielle couldn't seek help anywhere
And Mr. Zero knew this
So he decided to pursue this sick fantasy
Floorboards squeaking
Pleading for Danielle to flee
But Danielle wasn't dreaming
She was breathing...breathing... sharply
As he entered her room and climbed into her bed
Doing things he wasn't supposed to
His hands were so cold and he told her
It was either her, or her little sister
And that's when she became bolder
Mr. Zero would die before her touched her little sister
So her fists grew
And she proceeded to hit him kick him bite him fight him
Just enough to free herself
Little sis already in the hall crying
Danielle grabbed her hand and pulled her down the stairs
Running, running to her neighbor's house
Fists pounding, pounding till the door flew open
Arms reaching, reaching for Danielle and her little sister
Mr. Zero nowhere to be seen

So in the months to follow
Danielle became of model
Of what it looked like to succeed
She helped put Mr. Zero away in a cell to suffer the hell
He'd caused other girls her age
Mommy was still wife
And wife went to jail too
For not doing what a mother was supposed to
So granny took them in
Where Danielle would begin to heal
And be the best Danielle she could be

And now Danielle with a college degree is known as Ms. Danielle
And to the victims of rape she mentors she is
Ms. Hero
And to her loving husband she is
Mrs. Hero
And Mrs. Hero
Has triumphed over tragedy
She had to be
More than what she was expected to be
Preaching to girls around the world that
Mr. Zeros are not ok
And so today Mrs. Hero doesn't consider herself a hero

Just Danielle
But believe me when I tell you
She is

My Society, My Reality

Reach

Today I cried.
For the first time in months
My compressed depression bumped into my conscience
Consciously aware I wasn't paying good enough
attention
To my emotional ventilation left open by the last
emotional bout I had
It tainted my mindset
Which responded by allowing a lone tear
Pave a path of heart-wrenching images collected by my
eyes
Overflowing receptacles of bullshit I witness
But where's the judge to hear me testify?
Too consumed with paperwork and politics
To realize there's still blood on the ground
From the last stabbing of a young person's dreams
Clean up on aisle Forgotten

Today I cried.
Awakened by the salty taste of tear in the corner of
my mouth
Tongue searching for delectable dreams
But instead finding tasteless nightmares

I want to back track the browsing history
And delete this reality from my hard drive
Virus corrupting database of pain Jamal's mother felt
Burying her son is a low budget casket
Half the neighbors saddened
Other half just want to know what happened
Must have been slangin' or bangin'
Six feet under?
Nigga had to be
But nigga named Jamal just happened to be crossing
the street amidst a drive by
And his shell toe Adidas just couldn't move his body
fast enough
Away

I want to wipe this tear away
Maybe mail it to the media
So they can broadcast a solution
No more drama
I'll lend it to every offender of humanity
So they can stare into the reflections of their actions
Keep it, I'd say

But my hand just can't reach that high

Negativity elevated

Celebrated

Delegated to communities

Hate clouds rain down upon fruitless land

Nothing was going to flourish here anyway

That's what Alyssa's father said

Till bullshit rang true in the cavity of her innocence

Echoing off insults her father fed her mother

Too bruised, too scared to let go of the steering wheel

Of a broken down pinto of a family

So Alyssa ran aimlessly

From back seat, to mattress, to flat surface

Her back found its way there

Because compliments never found a way

Into the polluted airwaves of her environment

Fucked

Till the walls of her future were demolished by constant thrusts of memory

Her father's incessant complaints still squeak louder than the bed frame

Today I cried.

I cried because Jamal never got to
And Alyssa was never taught how
I cried
For everyone bred not to feel
And those killed before they got the chance

I want to reach
Take these hands and move the clouds of Heaven
Enough so the residents who checked in early
Can linger longer in the lobby of life

Take these hands
Dig up the mass grave of shattered dreams
Give them a proper burial
Let their remnants seep into the ground
So a new dream will one day bloom

I want to take these hands
Scoot Jamal down the street a little faster
To reach his destination
Not the casket
Bullets blasting back behind him

And for Alyssa

I'd wash her soul until it shined
Her self-esteem until it sparkled
Off her back and on her feet
Upright for the long run

I'd take these hands
Right these wrongs
And stop the bloodshed
Pass out confidence like handshakes
Firm grasp on life

But before I can do any of this
I will wipe this tear away
The problem is that my hand
Just can't reach high enough

Society's Mirror

We have thought and strived and leaped over obstacles
We curse and fight, but our thoughts are philosophical
We follow followers, and lead supposed leaders
We fight back tears of ignorance; our visions aren't clear
This day was yesterday, and the future is in the past
We can't move forward
We take steps we took last
And from blasts from the past
We see mistakes from history
Yet we repeat them and enable our own misery
Visionaries, leaders, prophets, and advocators
Can't stop and smell the roses cuz' opportunity will be by later
Our consciousness morphs into wants and desires
And to get what we what
We become murders and liars
Kids want to be grown
And live, and let live
Holding' guns and switchblades
Instead of toys and baby bibs
We breathe in negativity
We breathe out common courtesy

But our manners dissolve because we live in broken society
Our futures look bright
But our spirits become dimmer
As we finally take a look in society's mirror

Reflection

I peered into the mirror of society today
I found it lying in a gutter of lies and deceit
Wiped it clean with clarity and decided to take a peek
But my reflection transformed into a memory
Gorgeous, proud queen
Toasted almond skin
Head held high despite her crown
The butt of a rifle knocks it down
She picks it up off the ground
Told me to put it on, so I did
Her memory began to turn into his dream
A lost dream, cracked and shattered by the same whip that shattered and cracked his back
His Master said slaves can't dream
So he tossed it away for me to dream it for him, and I did
His dream turned into silence
Shh!! The hounds were on their trail
Momma and Baby, but Poppa lagged behind
Boot was stuck in the thick mud of the swamp
They told me not to worry
Just follow the stars, so I did
Their silence was broken with song
Rich, sorrowful spirituals
Bellowed from the soul

I absorbed every single verse and every single word
But their song became forced silence
I had to become their voice, so I did
With silence comes pain
He didn't mean to stare at her for so long
But her smile, he couldn't help but to glance
There was a gleam in his eyes as he stared her way
I struggled to imitate it
Like the men in white robes struggled to drag him out of the house
He gave me that same gleam in his eyes to remember him by, and I still do
Somewhere in the distance I heard laughter
I took a closer look and saw four little girls
Pointing and giggling in the church basement
They shared some of their contagious laughter with me before the explosion
I wanted them to look into the mirror with me
But they told me to look into it for them, so I did
Their giggles ceased and for a moment, I couldn't see anything
My eyes began to focus
I saw a tree
Something in the branches began to sway in the breeze
Amongst the blossoms and ripe berries were stems made of twine

This tree bore strange fruit
Blood on the leaves and blood on the roots
Not the scent of magnolias, but the stench of death
Spirits began to urge me to leave this strange crop
So I did
I decided to hold the mirror up to the sky
So my community, so society, so everybody could see
what I saw
Instead they began to pillage the past
They pawned her crown for a pistol
His dream for bling
Substituted their silence for the streets and their
song for slang
His gleam became a glare and their laughter became
tears
The strange fruit was forgotten in the same gutter I
found the mirror

Our history was not meant to be pillaged, but
preserved
Those before us sacrificed for us to succeed
Not to become selfish beings
We are kings and queens
We were told to dream, not miss opportunity
We are supposed to sing, not curse our community
Not destroy our society
I promised to remember our history, and I did

It's time to flourish, and grow, and succeed, and believe and dream and sing and laugh, and hope, and live and love
Because those before us couldn't
But in their name, we will

It's Time

It's time to realize that the civilized have already moved on
The procrastinators and waiters
The wanna-doers and stayers
Delay stepping up to the plate
Broken promises and half-thought dreams fall down in layers
And as we yell it's time
Time has already moved on
We've been waiting on our break so long
While others snatch up the plentiful and throw us the crumbs
Yet we say it's time?
No, time has passed us
Our foolishness has blinded us
Unfocused us
And led us to miss our chance
It's time to stop our speaking
And begin our plan in seeking
The bond to strengthen weakening
The cement to patch up leaking
No need to find our seating
'Cuz time can't wait for nobody
No, time won't wait for no one
Whether or not it's the right one

Discussion over 'cuz it's time!
To open up the government's curtains
Show them men, women, and children are hurting
And see the finger flirting with the trigger on the gun
It's time to end confusion
Instead of this finger pointing and choosing
Because one day you will see
That the time has already begun

The Home Front

Explosions...
Wake me from warm and delicious sleep
Rattling the ground from gutter to street
To corner...

This is not the place for sweet dreams
But absolute misery
Not the time for contemplation
But for revenge and hatred
For survival...

This is why I must fight
There's no time to serve my country
As a battle brews in my reality
Stepping out of my comfort zone
Swarmed by tragedy
Broken...mentally
Physically spent
Tripping over pacifiers and toys
As they line the street
Drunken men from the night grab at my feet
Pleading for more money, more liquor, more death
But I don't have time to give into wants and needs
As I drown in my own stupidity
Sputtering and choking on my own foolery

Filled in an ocean created by my own community
But there's no time for drowning
No time for floundering in a sea full of what ifs
No time to think of what could be
It's been an eternity since I've seen a dream
Not stampeded on but fulfilled
And still I must fight

Grab a gun grab a knife
Kill another to save your life
Take a wallet steal a car
Use the earnings of others to get far

Away
Running past broken street lights
And houses full of crack
Keep moving forward
Too scared to look back
To what happened last
When a future's not guaranteed
Who cares about the past?

I was given this task at birth
To fight hard, to fight day and night
Grab her neck take your knife
Hold it close scar her life
Grab the purse throw her down

Run off and dig down, down, down
Into her $20 Coach bag from a hustler on the block
Dig down down down down down and don't stop
To you reach her soul
Like the one you traded for a Glock
Dig down to her spirit
Yours is chained and locked
Dig down to her mind
Such a terrible thing you wasted
Dig down down down to her heart
Which you shattered apart

Take a soul
Steal a spirit
Get by for the day
Break a heart, neglect a mind
Throw your life away

But this is the life of a soldier
Not of a brigade but a hood
Not marching but running
Their purpose misunderstood
Not here to provide protection
Or serve a nation
This soldier represents a most tragic
Creation
Of governmental neglect and wishful thinking

As entire generations are literally sinking
In the wastelands of poverty and defeat
Creep, creep, creeping into the cribs of newborns
With preset destinies
Innocent adorable future ...· No bodies
Meant to serve one purpose... to fight
Crawl soldiers crawl
Climb soldiers climb
Walk soldiers walk
Run soldiers run
Limp soldiers limp
Stagger soldiers stagger
Die soldiers die
And let the next batch of almost some bodies rise
On your feet soldier on your feet
No time for sleep
As...

Explosions...
Wake me from warm and delicious sleep
Rattling the ground from gutter to street
To corner...

Hide your emotions hide your fear
Leave all caution behind when you near
The home front
Soldiers only

Detour to Feelings

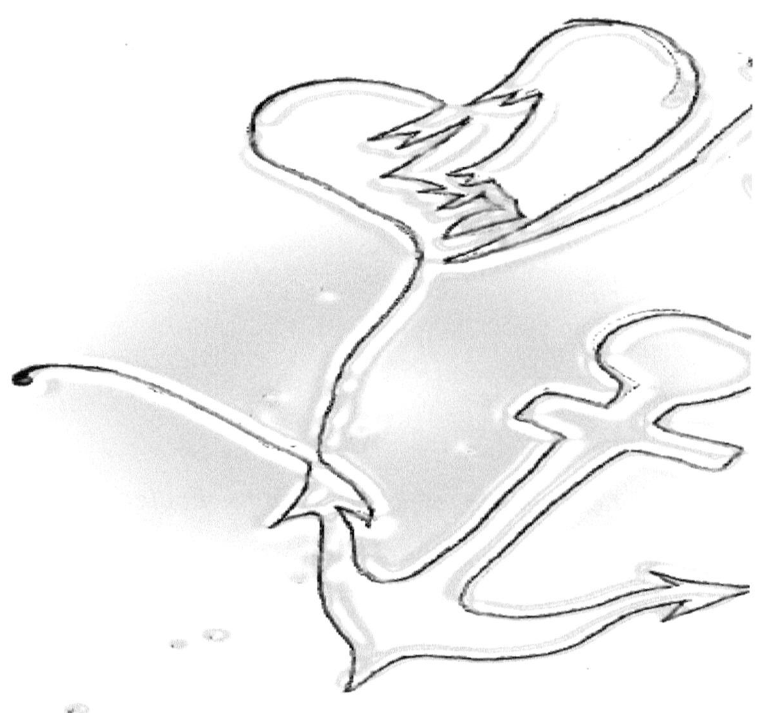

Appetite

May I devour your mind?
Your conversations are delectable
My mouth salivates chewing over responses
None of which can express my heart boiling over
In anticipation, well-seasoned with affection
You quench a thirst like no other.
Your essence saturates my skin like cool rain on a summer day, refreshing
I want to sip you slowly, savoring the sweet flavor
Licking the rim of the glass, slowly, surely, consuming every trace of you
Uncertain how to request a refill
You are my secret ingredient.
Every recipe before you has failed to transpire
Your aroma permeates the curtain of commonality
And makes love to my starving soul
Inspiring unknown flavors of pleasure
Dessert has never been so sweet.
My tongue searches for remnants of sugary verses past
Alas I come across a delectable treat
Hidden behind a tasteless dish past expiration
Each calorie worth every knee shaking memory
I have a purse full of sincerity to pay you.
Though the bill, I assume is beyond my compensation

And even as a savor your flavor amongst my taste buds
Please accept my heartfelt apology
For my insatiable appetite

I Want To

I want to move you
Towards unknown destinations we can discover together

I want to map you
Circumnavigate your landscape
And calculate the coordinates
Of your personal pleasure

I want to write you
Carve your stanzas into my soul
Consume your spoken word whole
As your inner thoughts leave a trail
I'll follow this sweet path without fail

I want to muse you
So paint me like Picasso
Play me like Hendrix
Sing me like Vandross
Then sign this masterpiece
With sheer ecstasy
So you and I can become a legacy

I want to ill you
Confining you to your bed

Your temperature rising exponentially
No cure for me in sight

I want to school you
Hold you after class
For disturbing my sanity
Keep you past your curfew with my wants
Punish you with my desires

Let me anchor you to satisfaction
No more warfare, just passion
Our hearts bound for infinity
I'll love you with the utmost tenacity

Careless Paint Strokes

It's forgotten like dreams interrupted, your love is
Fell somewhere between life's cushions
Or devoured by the sock monster in the dryer
Added to the pile of mis-mates, no match

What happened?

I remember painting you golden
With splashes of all shades of love
Took down old posters of boy bands past
And nailed you in the middle of my new beginning

I thought the house was sinking.

I'd rush downstairs to find my masterpiece tilted
As if I painted your eyes to look at the door that way
Readjustments equated confusion as you shifted back to imperfection
Or simply away from me

You robbed me.

You left and even took the nail I hung you on

The outline of your existence makes everything around me appear faded
Staring at this empty wall with a bag of expectations for supper, I'm speechless
You could have at least left me the nail

I robbed you.

I painted over your pre-existing canvas, colorblind
Placed you among my life's decor, no consultation
Swallowing my over-cooked fault across from your empty chair, I'm thankful
You loved me enough to stay that long.

I Want To Laugh

I would laugh but…·
Sorrow seems to make a better friend
My vision is continually distorted by fantasy
My mind races to turn it into reality
But it all collapses in the end

Why do I even bother?
I know things, many things
But I can't even begin to explain this, this…··**AHHH!!!**
What is this force that is strangling my heart?
Scissors in hand it is shredding my soul apart
Does it really matter?
I never seemed able to share it anyway…··

I'm worthy enough
I've struggled enough, bled enough
Damn it, I deserve as much
But what is such pain
Heart-wrenching, unbearable pain
Without sweet, desirable pleasure?

Just to be comforted
        It's okay…··
Be held
        Don't let go…··

Is it that my touch is cold?
Or that someone else's brings you more warmth?
Is it that my conversation is undesirable?
Or that melodies roll off her tongue and caress your eardrums?
I want to be more than just a thought
Let me be your inspiration!
You're the reflection seen in my conscience
Nourishment to my very being

I WANT TO LAUGH SO BAD!!!!

But the emptiness I feel is being magnified by the tears in my eyes
I want to laugh
But your name has yet to be added to my mental dictionary
Just let me smile
Just let me leap for joy....
But the heaviness I wear prevents me

I see possibilities
Piling up and waiting for us to rummage through
I hear the laughter
Oh-so-sweet laughter shared amongst one another

I taste the delectable candies we've exchanged on anniversaries past
I smell the subtle scent of fresh rain flowing through our open bedroom window
Caressing us as we tussle
Moaning our sweet ballads of......of love

But I can't feel you
I need to touch you

And without this I've come to the realization
That I may never be with you

So I sit pondering on the path set before me
As I step on yours I hesitate
Knowing that if I travel into your world
I may never find mine anymore
Just go...
Don't mind the thoughts of two etched in my mind for eternity
Just go...
Ignore the tear-stained cheeks
And that destiny herself is meek

Just know that I'm still standing idly on my path
And as I merge once more with my life
You can still find me

I'll be the girl with the biggest smile
Dreaming silently of you

The Game

You placed a bet on Lust
Pawns in position
Board crooked with ill intent
You roll the dice with confidence
Certain of the moves you wanted to make
But you forgot the rules
Passed Go before the game even began
Every player gets a turn
Even when you think you're steps ahead
You will never role a Perfect Me
I am the ultimate Get-out-of-jail-free
Except I choose to burn all chutes and ladders
I Declared War upon your misconstrued ideals
Go Fish for your shattered relationship
"I was just playing The Game" you say
I am too

King Me.

Finding Me

The Chronicles of Poetry

Understand me when I say this:
I love Poetry.

So much that I absolutely despise her
I want to dice her into little pieces
And serve her to the wordless
Verbless
Descriptionless
Strip her down to the bone
And throw the excess into thesaurical compost
As her rancid evil seeps into the Earth
So that in spring
Little bushels of bullshit litter the fields of what used to be
Absolute, silent tranquility

Understand me when I say this:
I absolutely hate Poetry

To the point that I can't help but to embrace her
So graceful as she pirouettes in my mind
Leaps in my soul
And spins around like she owns it
Because she does
Every syllable of her takes a bow
After such a miraculous performance

But I want to enjoy more of her
Write odes of her very existence
And SCREAM her to the Heavens
So that the angels can be moved too
But she keeps running offstage as the curtain closes
Ignoring encouragements for an encore
Breaking my heart

That BITCH!
So I threw the roses in the gutter
And let the balloons fly in the air
I don't care
Because I used to dream of Poetry
Yet only now it's a painful nightmare
Blackness surrounds me
Blacker than Death
Death…
The Death of Poetry…

I crave Poetry so much
That in order to live
She must die…

I want her to burn

I want to scorch her very existence
Pouring flammable language within her context

And leave her sizzling in the distance

I want to destroy her

Until her vowels melt into constantans
Then punctuation
Then nothingness
Running into the gutter
For the rodents to feed upon
And mutate into vicious lyrical creatures
Only to explode and splatter
Poetic matter across the world
Their veins too feeble to contain the acidic nature of poetry

But as I walk towards her
Lighter in hand
She suddenly reaches out
Pulling my ears to her lips and says:
"I need you".

She grasps the furniture
Struggling to stand on Her own 2 vowels
And I extend my helping hand
Aware that my future is intertwined in Her chaotic past

I lead her
Past fragments and question marks and red ink
Into the library of my soul
She skims through my collection of dreams
Stumbling across images of Her and I running together
Freely
No structure or end rhyme necessary
She spots my memory bank
And begins depositing her funds into my account
So that I may benefit from the wealth of her wisdom
And I promise not to withdraw in fear of a negative balance

But fear won't let go of me
I excuse myself and run nonstop to the outer banks of my soul

And there I find her... My Poetry lifeless....
And I fooled by an imposter...

So what are you waiting for?
Gazing into this empty coffin
What more do you want of her?
She…didn't…deserve….
THIS!
But you…

You are not innocent victims
But soulless bystanders
Her screams interrupting the tunes of your stupidity
But you turn them up louder

As these poets begin to pound her
Until her screams become whimpers
and her whimpers become silence
And you silently walk away
She… didn't… deserve… this

And yet you insist on watching her dangled like strange fruit
Her blood on the leaves and upon the roots
Her subtle scent, now an outrageous stench
A death unexpected yet imminent

You sit here today to mourn her
Try scorning Her
Burn Her remainders and tell each other She never existed
Strip Her from the history books
And ban schools from teaching Her
Paint over Her content with nonsense
Scribble over Her undeniable spirit
With your irrelevant bullshit

Beat Her till She's unresponsive
Tie bricks to her hands and feet
And toss Her into a river of selfishness
When Her lifeless verses wash upon shore
Bury Her in Her own embarrassment
And feed your children with the produce of this vile compost

She was my definition
My last breath
My final heartbeat
And you've destroyed her
So tell me..
Who the hell am I supposed to be?

Whispers

And she whispers…
Sweetly, softly
Tossing hues of happiness into a colorless reality
Broken skies projecting memory and tragedy

But she whispers…
Quiet unknowns blaring in my reality
Unraveling my sanity
For all of eternity
And she whispers
Sweet nothings
Anything
Something like I love you
And I miss you
And everything's okay
Pieces of childhood sprinkled across servings of pain
Disdain accompanies the rain
Or tear streaks
Whichever occurs first
Reflecting recollections of remembrance
Perched upon the weariness of my soul

And I SCREAM
I LOVE YOU…· like life
Like wonderment and discovery

I MISS YOU...

Like split second reactions and happily ever afters
How am I supposed to master
Heartache and broken dreams
Without hugs and understanding
Forever branded
By history
Better known as misery
Blurry images of everything we never had a chance to be
Blocked out
Present but unaware
As you stare at things that aren't there
Unspoken being outspoken in your mind
And I find myself distorted in a wrinkle in time
And in this wrinkle I'm imprisoned
From visions of freedom that you promised me

And you mumble
Unintelligent rants
And I can't understand anymore
Pounding on glass walls
I can't through anymore
Mommy I don't know what to do anymore

And you whisper...
I love you

And I miss you
And everything's okay
But Mommy you're so far away
Tunnel after tunnel leading nowhere
And I travel these dark passage ways
Hoping to stumble on remnants of you
Kicking aside what ifs and never wills
And still
You're invisible

I want to see
You
Staring in the mirror
Rubbing your tummy
Wondering who exactly I would eventually be
Planning new discoveries and opportunities
Your hands running over an unborn me
And you stand
Barefooted
Belly protruding
Headscarf cruising around plaited hair
And your stare
Past reflections
Towards the future
And you whisper...
I love you
And everything's okay

But today

Mommy I whisper…

I miss you

Prostitute of Poetry

Sometimes I feel like a prostitute of poetry.
I was introduced to the game in the 7th grade.
Some said I was too young to take part in such things
But my teacher assured me that the clients liked 'em young
But first I had to learn the basics
I couldn't just go up there, she said
I had to step sensually up to the mic
And slowly adjust it, just a little
Speak ever so softly so that the clients would lean in
Suddenly speaking louder
Quicken the flow of my verses until the room begins to spin
The lights become brighter, the temperature climbs higher
My heart beats faster, and faster, and faster
Until everything, in the room, the city, the sky, on earth
Suddenly, slowly, starts to fade away…
I couldn't just go up there, she said

Besides I had to figure out what my specialty would be
Every working poet had a thing
I could be a bubble gum poet

You know, the one who chews up the truth to blow more lies
Weaving a web of deceit to complete their disguise
Just when the clients shout, "Wait! Don't stop!"
The bubble of chaos can do nothing but...pop
But my mother always told me blowing bubbles in public wasn't polite
So instead, I tried being a poet of the limelight
The one who has been everywhere, but ain't been anywhere
They get a little air beneath their wings and think they're flying high
But unplug the fans and watch their ego deflate and die

But I had a perpetual fear of heights
And with no act, I had no show
Who knew it would be so hard to stoop so low
To become a master of lyrics of the tongue
Especially designed to caress the client's eardrums
And if the client didn't like my sound
My words would simply fall to the ground
Absorbed by the pavement to be stepped on another day
Keep in mind, I have bills to pay
And dreams require cash

But the only thing selling these days are verses referring to my...
Actually anything that degrades me
But makes the clients go crazy
As the room becomes hazy
With chaos, lies, and shady
Poets, who aren't poets but imposters
Raping spoken word
Until the syllables begin to bleed
Talking about what poetry did for them that day
Not mentioning exactly how they preserved poetry for the poets to come
But... it ***HAS*** *to be poetry*
It ***HAS*** *to be a masterpiece*
Because the clients are hoopin' and hollerin' and the clients ***NEVER*** *lie*
Yes, the audience is screamin' and shoutin'
And couldn't possibly lie

But YOU mentally deny
Truth, reality, life
What I present to you today is not a performance
I am not here to entertain you
I am not here to please you
I am here to inform you
You can cover your ears and close your eyes
But your soul, your spirit

Can do nothing but open wide
Taking in pain
Pain that never lies as it thrives inside
I do not desire the prize of your hand clap
Nor a trophy of compliments
Don't reward me with courtesy
You can save that for the poets of the limelight
I do not have a specialty
At least, none for your eyes
There is not a magical mic in my pocket or a pleasant surprise
What I offer you is my word
What you have before you is me
Sometimes I feel like a prostitute of poetry
But I'm not trapped in mental bankruptcy
You can cash in all the hand claps you want
But it will never be worth my dignity

Life

Life is funny.
With its twists and turns
And rain when it's sunny
And its cracks that trip you up
The ones that can't always be filled up
But with these imperfections
Life can be as sweet as honey
But with a sour aftertaste
Sometimes it slows down
But it can certainly make haste
No life's a waste
Because this life affects the next
And that life does the same
And if each life is a player
Then we've made a game
And from the first two players
Came a whole world of contestants
Some who jump at an opportunity
And some who are hesitant
But each player's moves can affect another's
Life can produce possibilities and dead ends
And no one's given instructions on how to play
Yet and still your moves affect a life of tomorrow
And those around you today

Know Thyself

Know Thyself?
How can I even know myself?
A shattered life separates me from myself
And to no one I belong
See, my life has been slashed
Dream mashed, soul bashed
Lashed with rage and frustration
What's supposed to be one of life's most wonderful creations
Has managed to be trapped in lost and found
No memory of what was
Unable to make a sound
Because as I open my mouth, my heart jumps in my throat
As my insecurities gaze at what I wrote
And let's note
That I myself am lost
And no one has stated the cost
The cost of finding me
So whatever was locked in me
Has disappeared along with me
The possibilities that flowed through me

Will never ever have the chance to see
What I, it, and everything could be
Because to find me
Would mean becoming lost in me
And seeing that I know not of me
I could never dream of anything
Except being anything but me

About the Author

Born and raised in Milwaukee, Wisconsin, Jessica Holden learned early on the meaning of survival. After being neglected by her mother who suffers from Schizophrenia, Holden was placed in foster care for nine years. During this time, she used writing and academics to cope with her life.

Jessica now attends Northwestern University majoring in Learning and Organizational Change and has received over $50,000 in scholarships and awards. She is an active member of Zeta Phi Beta Sorority, Incorporated, and spends her time volunteering, being with friends and family, and advocating for the rights of children in foster care.

www.ingramcontent.com/pod-product-compliance
Ingram Content Group UK Ltd.
Pitfield, Milton Keynes, MK11 3LW, UK
UKHW041920190726
13854UKWH00003B/1345

9 781105 685231